PRESENTED BY BELINDA JOHNSON

FITNESS
SHIFT!

**Intimate Journeys of Women Who Shifted
Their Destiny Through Fitness.**

Fitness Shift!
by Belinda Johnson
Copyright 2016 by Belinda Johnson

ISBN-13: 978-1539521068
ISBN-10: 1539521060

Dedication

This book collaboration is dedicated to the
courageous women who has and will embrace
their destiny to create a Fitness SHIFT!

Contents

Introduction

As I sat in my bed with my laptop, pen and paper, I pondered about which life event I should share in this introduction. As I reflected on my life, tears started streaming down my face. Something was different about these tears. My tears were no longer tears of sorrow but tears of JOY. For so many years I cried tears of sorrow because of losses, broken relationships, low self-esteem, you name it. Just thinking about those times put me in a position to REJOICE because all things are NEW!

With that being said, I spoke to myself softly and said, "Hmmm." Maybe I will tell them about the time when I found myself in a very unhealthy relationship with a man who was abusive mentally, emotionally, and verbally. I entered into a relationship in which I played the role of a helpless victim. Being manipulated and deceived, I allowed the toxic relationship to spill over until it affected every area of my life. Depressed, disappointed, and down-right miserable, I became what some may call an angry black woman. Living with that type of deception, verbal abuse, and manipulation, my strength was depleted, and so was my desire to do anything right mentally and physically.

One day, I ended up in a parking lot with this man who uttered these words directly into in my ear, "I will put this knife to your throat and cut you to death." I remembered saying to myself while this was happening, "This must come to an end." All I knew at that moment was I wanted out, and my life was worth living. I spoke these words to myself, "I WANT OUT, SO I CAN HELP OTH-ERS AND SHOW THEM A BETTER WAY OF LIFE!" This was the beginning of my giving birth to Coach BFIT.

As I was thinking about this significant life-changing event, I couldn't help but remember that even though I was in what appeared to be a helpless situation, God sent the most amazing person across my path to rescue me with unconditional love. This particular person started to pour words of wisdom into me that helped build my confidence, regain self-love, learn to trust again, and shift my perspective on life. It wasn't that I was a bad person, I just made some bad decisions that cost me more than I had bargained for. I was always settling by placing myself on the back burner and doing for others, while neglecting to tend to my own well-being. I became keenly aware of three things while in this toxic relationship:

1. Toxic relationships kill your drive from being who you are supposed to be.

2. Unhealthy relationships rob you of strength to perform your purpose and be the individual you were called to be.

3. Your health is inhibited and destroyed from having the optimal state of being when you continue in an unhealthy relationship.

Although I made some foolish decisions in my life that yielded some bad consequences, God still met me at each event with His loving arms stretched out beckoning me to come to Him. The more I would trust Him, the less I would settle for things that meant me harm. I began to remove anything that negatively impacted my life, aside from just people. I identified everything from foods which didn't nourish my body, activities that drained me, and every person who was not meant to be a part of my SHIFT. I learned to trust in people again, live a liberated life, and allow love to find me in a healthy place mentally, spiritually, and physically. That person who crossed my path during my healing process is now my husband, who I call (My Chocolate Drop), Eric Cornell, of fourteen years. He was graced to handle me in my ugly stage, my in-between stage, or my confused stage. You name it. He had the strength to handle me with love, care, and "tough love," I might add.

In the midst of the various seasons in my life disappointments, unbearable pain, hurt, confusion, and bad doctor reports, I discovered my purpose. I came to the conclusion that every event in my life, whether good or bad, made up the totality of who I am today. Now, I use every part of my story to rescue others from a place in their life that is dormant, debilitating, or toxic by way of fitness. I am the voice of "Fitness" that coaches others into a healthier place in life physically, mentally, or spiritually.

My question to you is, "What is hindering you from SHIFTING into a New Season of life that will bring about a positive change in every area of your life- mentally, physically, spiritually, and financially?" Whether it is low self-esteem, a lack of self-control with eating, your past, laziness, etc., know that CHANGE IS POSSIBLE. As you begin to read every chapter in this book, allow your heart to be open to change. You may find yourself in these stories, and when you do, allow your confidence to be awakened to another level, and embrace the "shift." Get Ready, IT'S ABOUT TO BE A FITNESS SHIFT!

Belinda Bfit Johnson

I plan to make my shift by:

_____

_____

_____

_____

_____

_____

_____

_____

_____

_____

_____

_____

_____

_____

1

Belong Believe Become

"Being healthy isn't temporary; it's a lifetime."
—Brenda Henderson

Thirty-eight years ago, when my mother died a young woman of age 40, my idea of health was tied to anxiety and not education. In my mind, I felt that it would not be long before I met the same fate. I was 27 years old.

My thoughts of living forever like most others my age turned into bad dreams with thoughts of not living to 40 years old was constant.

I had no health challenges nor had any doctor informed me of anything other than I was in good health, but when I went to sleep at night my subconscious took me to places I did not want to visit.

During the late 70's and early 80's health messages were quite different than they are today.

During that period many people who had parents and siblings to pass at an early age expected that they too would not have longevity.

The worst time of the day became my bedtime. I hated it because no matter how tired I was or whether I went to bed early or late as soon as I got into a deep sleep the bad dreams would began.

I either became very ill in these dreams or I was in an accident of some sort. There was always some type of catastrophe.

I would awaken from these dreams for a few minutes but as soon as I went back to sleep they would all start again.

Every new disease or condition that was published I thought is this something that's going to change my life would enter my head. Soon these conditions were added to the dreams.

I spent a lot of time at doctor's visits that only resulted in good health reports but that did not stop the pinned up fears.

The fears were like roller coaster rides. Some times these fears were intense and other times I was able to coast along. I spent so much time hiding these fears from everyone around me.

I never looked forward to birthdays during this period, the closer it got to them the dreams would get worse and wipe me out resulting sometimes to anxiety attacks. I was afraid the tragedies in these dreams would take me out days prior to the next big day.

After years of tormenting myself with these dreams and fears, a friend out of the blue asked me if I was interested in improving my life expectancy and I immediately replied yes but at the same time I was thinking has this person been in my dreams. How in the world did he know I had not shared those concerns and fears with a single soul? What is up with this?

After getting caught up in all my emotions and trying to figure out how I got exposed, I almost missed the later part of the conversation, which was an invite to attend a briefing on the subject.

All that night and the next day, I was on edge about what the meeting could be about. What could they tell me about all of my worries?

The evening came. I arrived to this quaint townhouse and once entering I did not know a soul so my secrets were safe until the doorbell rang. I saw one of my relatives entering and immediately put myself in shut down mode.

Okay, what kind of meeting is this and how much information do I have to share because I truly did not want my secrets to be let out the bag.

Well, the clock struck seven and the meeting began. A man stood in front of the room, introduced himself and welcomed everyone that attended. He began to ask questions such as: Whose interested in improving their health,? Who would like to live longer? As hands were raised, I immediately thought "Do all these folks have the same problem as I do?"

After listening to him recite what seemed like a twenty-six volume encyclopedia of health statistics I started to relax a bit. I said to myself "I am in the right place."

That night, I was not only introduced to the Dick Gregory Bahamian Diet but also to a whole new mindset on being healthy.

From the seminars, webinars and conferences I began to learn so much. Things such as: the importance of eating fruit and vegetables, how animals are handled, how foods are processed in this country, where our food supply comes from, what is put in the foods that are labeled as preservatives, as well as how pollutants, chemicals, pesticides effect our foods, the importance of exercise and so much more.

It was during these times I began believing there was a possibility I could live longer than 40 and be healthy and strong as well.

I began researching, reading, and listening to everything I could on healthy living.

From the fact-finding, I began to shift my way of living, which can be hard especially if your family is use to their routines and years of habits.

One of the first changes I made was to become a semi-vegetarian. I gave up red meat and pork and began eating just chicken and seafood. Living in Virginia, the pork capital of the US , plus residing about twenty minutes from Smithfield Foods where all the pork products such as country bacon and Virginia ham is processed.

From there I began touting healthy living everywhere. I began sharing my newfound knowledge with family, co-workers, friends, and anyone who would listen.

By no means was it an easy task because everything I was learning about being healthy, there was always someone who had a rebuttal or some sort of disbelief, which was sometimes hard for me to understand. It seemed like I was totally in this lane all by myself. After about two years of not eating meat I became an anemic. My physician recommended that I return to eating meat. This is when all of the backlash from doubters began especially from those who were the closest to me. I was down for a while, feeling as if I were betraying all I had learned.

Thank God the network of friends I made on this new journey kept me encouraged. I maintained my discipline of staying on track, while at the same time realizing that all of what I was doing was for me and I had to continue for me. I also had to accept that this was my journey and not theirs. They had not been in my head and they knew nothing about what I had been feeling. Therefore, I had to keep this whole journey well balanced.

After being affiliated with five direct sales companies whose emphasis were on being healthy after my introduction to the Bahamian program, my belief in myself as well as the impact of what I was doing began to evolve. Co-workers, friends, and family made me their go-to person asking for information on how they could change their lifestyles.

I now knew I was on my way to becoming not only a great source of information, but also an inspiration to the change of lifestyle they were seeking.

It seemed like everywhere I went I was running into folks who were either asking me what was I selling to improve the quality of life or what I was doing to maintain my good health.

In 2014, after arming myself at a conference focused on a new medical breakthrough, the universe directed me in the development of my company Health Boss.

I was already sharing with many, so why not develop a business where I could reach more people. My motto became: *Learn How To Be Healthy At Any Age.* Development of this company has lead to speaking at health fairs, and meetings with groups wanting information on what they can do to become healthy.

I use my platform as a resource to those who are seeking information as well as healthy recipes and health tips.

I have also had the opportunity to share this passion with many as a freelancer of health articles and interviews of medical professionals for the following publications:

Supernaturally Fabulous Magazine, Emerge Magazine, ACHI Magazine, SizeOverated, Magazine Care Novate Magazine, and Health Journal Magazine. I also host the blog-talk radio show Health Talk with The Health Boss where we talk everything Healthy.

My journey of being and maintaining good health is not and will not be without challenges. You have each day to arm your mindset with something inspiring to keep you going. I often tell folks "being healthy is not temporary, it is a lifetime". As a favorite song of mine says "we fall down but we get up get back up again". That is what maintaining good health is all about.

If I had not changed the mindset I had 38 years ago I would still be living with fears and doubts of my health as well as my mortality. I probably would still fear sleeping and dreaming, instead I have shifted my life and the lives of others and have gone from being a member of the fearful unhealthy club to the Health Boss.

I plan to make my shift by:

_____

_____

_____

_____

_____

_____

_____

_____

_____

_____

_____

_____

_____

_____

2

Can I Hear Me Now?

*"Start now. Start with fear. Start with pain. Start
with doubt. Start with hands shaking. Start with voice
trembling but start. Start and don't stop. Start where you
are, with what you have. Just...start."*

—CHIQUITA BAXTER

If the "me" of my teenage and early adult years could see me now,
she'd be proud!

She would declare: *I'm so proud of you for standing up for yourself!
You are beautiful, smart, funny and brave!*

I have come out of a life filled with abuse, depression and loneliness. The younger me was overwhelmed with life. Every day was a
struggle for survival.

It was because of that lonely, depressed, and awkward little girl
on the inside of me that I began my personal journey of self-discovery, which I continue to this day.

I am no longer depressed or lonely, and I have a life-transforming story to tell!

At the age of twelve, I became a victim of domestic violence, by
my son's father. He repeatedly raped me, beat me and assaulted me
with vulgarity, telling me I was worthless and would never amount
to anything. I became pregnant by him at fifteen, but that did not
stop the beatings or the verbal abuse.

After years in that violent relationship, I finally found the courage to break free from the abuse - at least the physical part of it. However, I left that relationship only to find myself in other relationships that were just as verbally abusive. I felt loneliness and rejection. I internalized all the negative things that were being spoken over me. Part of me was missing and I cried out for help, but no one was listening.

In 2011, I was at the lowest point in my life. I wanted to commit suicide. I took a few extra sleeping pills here and there, hoping to never wake up. I was in so much pain and wanted out of my misery.

I hated everything about myself and never looked at myself in the mirror. I intentionally avoided taking pictures because I did not want to look at the ugly girl in the photos. I always found something wrong with me. My nose was too long. My cheek bones were too high. I was too fat. My legs were too thin, or my hair was not long enough. There was always something imperfect about me.

The pain grew worse as I got older. I could not love myself so I looked for love in all the wrong places. My depression grew darker, and the pain went deeper. It was overwhelming. I was so angry and mad at the world.

Added to that were marital problems and the stress I felt from my family. I love my family, and I know they love me, but I always felt "boxed in" by them. They had certain expectations of me. I was not allowed to fail or voice how I felt.

I desperately wanted to find my voice and my place in this world and to stop living for everyone else. After trying to deal with the issues unfolding in my marriage, I decided, for the first time, to stand up for myself.

I strongly believe that things happen for a reason. I believe God puts us in certain situations to teach us, mold us, and equip us for things to come. The issues I dealt with from the time I was twelve until I turned thirty-five in 2011, were preparing me for a radically different life to come.

What came next was exactly what I needed to turn my life around.

In 2011, a childhood friend, whom I had not seen in years, was home visiting family. We became Facebook friends and I shared with him my unhappiness with my life and with my physical appearance. He ran every morning and invited me to go running with him one day. Though he did not think I was overweight, he told me that running or exercise could help me deal with my issues and he encouraged me to start a fitness program. After he returned home, I took his advice and purchased a gym membership and hired a personal trainer.

I had no idea what to expect, and this new discipline was totally different than anything I had previously experienced. It was hard at first, but as I consistently pursued fitness, it shifted my destiny. I lost a few pounds and became stronger, but the most noticeable change came in the form of the confidence I gained. I now wanted to live! Did I just say that? Amazingly, YES! I wanted to LIVE!

I felt better when I ran and exercised. Physical activity took away my sadness. It helped me release my anger and my frustration. I needed the regimen of the gym and workouts. It SAVED my life. I felt myself becoming stronger mentally and physically. It was also cleansing - an emotional release. I cried a lot during that time and was finally able to let go of feelings of inadequacy and deal with the painful memories of abuse and rape.

In the past, I had sought treatment for my depression, but I never got better. The medication the doctors had prescribed made me feel terrible. I did not like how I felt, so I eventually quit taking it. As a result, my depression went untreated for several years.

Exercise became therapeutic for me. It was the only "antidepressant" I knew that worked. When I exercised it made me feel better about myself and about life in general.

My life of desperation was the catalyst for the journey I am on now. Exercise became my outlet to overcome depression. It was the only time I could shut out the world and concentrate on building myself up, so I pushed myself to the limit in my workouts. My doctor had told me I was borderline obese for my height, and my blood pressure was out of control. That kept me pushing toward a healthier lifestyle, and I started shedding pounds.

Though it was hard, I left the gym with a feeling of accomplishment. I was finally in control of my life. My confidence was soaring, and that confidence spilled over into my life outside the gym.

I was pleased with my growth through fitness. It had helped me confront the insecurities and issues I had dealt with for so long. I was grateful to my friend who had encouraged me to pursue fitness and continued to cheer me on from hundreds of miles away.

Even though I was becoming more confident and strong, I still could not look at myself in the mirror, so I decided to ACT, and I came up with a plan to help me overcome that issue. Since I knew that fitness was helping to change my life, I made the decision to take selfies at the gym and post them on Facebook. That choice forced me to look at myself in photographs.

I was no longer looking for approval from others but I needed to become more comfortable when sharing my photographs. My desire was to both help myself and share my journey with others. I hoped it would help them change their lives as it had mine.

Of course, there were days that I wanted to give up and did not want to get out of bed. I still have those days. The difference now is that I've learned how to confront my issues. I have realized that a mirror is not a reliable source from which to gain self-worth. God's word confirms that. It tells us: "Do not let your adorning be merely external" (1 Peter 3:3-4).

We have mistakenly relied on the mirror to tell us we're beautiful. I could have avoided a lot of pain and struggles if I had known this scripture earlier in life. I want others who are dealing with the same issues I have to recognize their strength and beauty, both inside and out. Fitness and self-love can help them on that journey.

If you think there is no way you can overcome the struggles and insecurities you face, I want to challenge you to start taking responsibility for your life and your happiness. Listen to your inner voice.

I eliminated those people in my life who were not good for me, along with any negative influences. I embraced those who encouraged and uplifted me, along with those things that had a positive influence on me. I reinforced my life through positive affirmations. Eventually, I was able to cope better with my depression. I learned to listen to my inner voice, and I discovered how important self-love was to survival.

For me, self-love meant being kind to myself by listening to my needs, creating boundaries and intentionally accepting and loving every part of me, from the top of my head to the soles of my feet.

Here are some of the steps I took that helped me to begin my journey:

Face it. The first step to creating change is to face your issues. I found the most helpful way to do that was to start journaling. You were never created to live in depression, defeat, guilt, shame or with feelings of unworthiness. You were created to be VICTORIOUS!!

Deal with it. Create a plan of action to help you deal with your insecurities.

ACT! You can journal all you want, but only action brings about change.

Let it out. Exercise is an outlet to boost your confidence, deal with stress, or overcome depression. Love yourself enough to start exercising. It is never too early or too late to work toward being the healthiest you can be.

We believe and internalize what we tell ourselves. As a man thinks, so is he...(Prov. 23.7)

It starts in the mind. Remember, death and life are in the power of our tongues (Prov. 18.21). Our words are powerful! Negative words and criticism assault our souls and block our ability to hear truth. If you have been criticizing yourself for years, and have no self-worth, begin encouraging and affirming yourself and watch what happens! Go someplace quiet, by yourself and without distractions. Have ears to hear what God says about you and get in agreement with Him, speaking the same things. Listen to that inner voice and let it guide you. Can I Hear Me Now? YES!

Chiquita Baxter is a Health and Fitness Enthusiast, Self-Love Coach, Fitness Apparel Designer and Founder of Girl On Her Game Enterprises. Her website is www.girlonhergame.com; email: chiquita@girlonhergame.com; Facebook, Instagram and Periscope handle is girlonhergame and Twitter: girlonhergame2.

I plan to make my shift by:

_____

_____

_____

_____

_____

_____

FITNESS
SHIFT PASS
FITNESSSHIFT.COM

"DESTINY BECKONING
WITH AN OUT-STRETCHED
HAND LOOKS A LOT
LIKE DECISION AND
DETERMINATION."

Cynthia Johnson

cynthia@tscmservices.net

3

There Are No Excuses Greater Than My Destiny

"There are NO excuses greater than my destiny."
—Cynthia Johnson

I've always struggled with the shape of my body. From the time I can remember, body image has always been an issue for me. As a youth, I was not considered obese, but I carried most of my excess weight in my hips and thighs. I've always wanted to have more of **an** athletic build, not curvy with big hips. Everyone who I thought was beautiful had long, lean legs, small hips, and small waist. No magazine models ever looked like me.

By the time I was 16, I thought I was a freak. On the top I was small, with small breasts and a small waist. My super-wide hips had their own thing going on and looked as if they belonged to someone else. Oh how I wished they didn't belong to me! My measurements were 34, 24, 42 and I weighed 136 lbs. The Commodores, an R&B group back in the day had a popular song called "Brickhouse" describing a woman with perfect body measurements of 34, 24 ,36. My hips were 6 inches too big for me to be a Brickhouse! I would kill for those numbers now (weight and measurements), but as a teenager in the 1980's, I was not happy with my body. I longed to look like everybody else. I spent a lot of time in the mirror pulling and pushing on the ample fat around my hips and butt. If only I could get rid of these blasted hips, I would be perfect. I wore dresses all the time to hide my hips and refused to wear shorts.

As a youngster in my pre-teens, I remember playing recreational softball. I was not the best athlete but I was pretty good at softball. I played the catcher's position behind home plate. It was the second or third inning when I overheard boys heckling behind me. I tried to focus on the pitcher and the batter, but I couldn't. Instead, I hung onto every word they said. I wanted to run away, to get as far away from their jokes, laughs and slick comments. My feelings were really hurt and I wanted the game to be over. I did not care who won, I just wanted it over. It is one of my most horrendous experiences. That night was my last time playing softball. I quit the team with no explanation to anyone. I never wanted to relive that encounter or anything similar to it. However, I did relive it. Men and women both voiced their opinions about my body. I am sure behind my back, but most times while standing directly in front of me. "You got a big ole butt!" People thought it was ok to tell me how different my body was shaped and how odd it was that I did not look like everyone else. Over and over again, comment after comment, the years chipped away at my self-esteem and confidence.

After graduating from high school, I did something no one else in my family had done. I joined the Air Force. My uncle had served in the Army during the Vietnam war, but I was the first to don the blue uniform and head off into the wild blue yonder. I boarded the Greyhound bus in Vidalia, Georgia and headed to the military processing station in Jacksonville, Florida. It was a new world for me and I was happy to be just one in the number. My happiness was short lived. I had grown accustom to sly comments about my body, but I had not encountered direct insults from strangers who took no account of my feelings. It was late in the evening when we arrived at Lackland Air Force Base, Texas. They had separated us into groups of about 30 and ushered us to our perspective day-rooms. We were instructed to sit on the floor, since we had not earned the right to sit in chairs. The Training Instructor (TI) walked in and began to bark out instructions with some details of what we had to look forward to over the course of the next 6 weeks. I was taking it all in and thinking "this isn't too bad". people hollered all the time where I'm from. I was lost in my own thoughts when the TI's glaring eyes fell on me. He looked at me and told me to stand up, my world stopped. Looking me up and down, he barked, "how much do you weigh?" I was mortified! I was so embarrassed I could not remember how much I weighed. I stood there, frozen. I couldn't think. I thought I was going to pass out. I tried to say something, anything to make it stop. I could hear myself mumbling 130 something, but I was not sure what I said. I did not recognize my own voice. "What?" the TI yelled. "Well, you are going to be one of my road guards, let's see if we can run some of that fat off of you!" And run, I did! For the next 6 weeks of basic training, I was a road guard running from the back of my flight with a water canteen strapped around my waist. I can still hear the TI yelling -road guards out! And I would come barreling from the rear of the formation to stand with my hand extended to stop traffic. Afterwards, I would run back to my position. I ran so much, that 6 weeks later I was almost 20 lbs. lighter. I guess that old TI's ultimate plan of trimming the fat worked. That experience happened over 30 years ago. I would feel the sting of that encounter and similar ones for many years to come. During my 21-year tenure in the military, I constantly fought to maintain weight standards. I had 4 of my 5 babies while on active duty. Baby after baby, the military weight standards were increasingly difficult for me to achieve. I would struggle and starve myself until eventually I would lose enough weight to make it back in my military uniforms. My hips and butt were always my problematic areas. Although I had become to enjoy exercising, the fat around my hips and butt kept me from having the body I really wanted.

My real test with my weight came with my 5th baby. I gained a whopping 80 lbs and topped the scales at 232 lbs. I was 43 and in the early stages of menopause. I tried my best to lose weight, but nothing seemed to work. I thought I would be able to spring back into the gym, and the weight would come off, but it did not. Five years after delivery, I was still close to 200lbs. I was border-line depressed and exhausted. My body was older, slower and fatter than I had ever been. I tried all sorts of weight loss gimmicks and fad diets only to give up when I could not maintain the super low caloric intake and strict diet plans. I tried my best not to succumb to unhealthy foods, but I could not maintain any diet plan for a sub-stantial period. I would always cave. I needed to understand why I could not commit myself long enough to see the results I longed to achieve. Sitting quietly one day, I began to meditate on my eating habits and lack of discipline. It was not intentional; I just let my mind drift, stopping only to take inventory of my emotions when I thought about denying myself food. What I discovered shocked me. My mind went back to a very difficult time in my childhood. My step-father worked for the local milling company in my small town and was critically injured on the job. That injury put him in the hospital and recovery for several months. During those times, my mother, my four sisters and I spent many days with very little food to eat. I remember as a little girl feeling like I was going to die. I did not understand hunger pains, but there were times I would feel sick because I was so hungry. The experience left an insidious imprint, one that had controlled my eating habits most of my adult life.

Something clicked for me when I realized this truth about myself. Somehow I had managed to bury these hardships deep in my subconscious, but those thought patterns controlled everything

I felt about food. The first thought I had to get rid of was that I was not going to die. I had to tell myself when I felt hungry that I was not going to die. It was a difficult transition. But slowly, I began to see change, not only in my body but in the way I felt about food. For the first time in my life, I was eating healthy with consistency. My body and the numbers on the scale began to change.

Throughout this tumultuous journey, my husband Howard has been my biggest supporter and cheerleader! As a Marine, he may take offense to being called a cheerleader, but his encouragement was unrelenting, and he simply would not let me fail. He always complimented me, even at my heaviest weight. I will always love him for that. He assured me that my goals for my body were attainable. I have a tremendous support team! My daughter, Najla helped me to run again. As an avid athlete, I would watch her run soccer sprints on the treadmill. I did not think I would ever run fast again. At least. not on this side of heaven! The first time I climbed on the treadmill to run I was super nervous about my knees, ankles, hips, etc. She would say start slow and stay close to the bar. I think she was worried about me potentially flying off the back end. Over time, I was able to increase my speed. I am now running sprints up to 9.0! Just 30 seconds long, but I am running!

My trainer, Hammed, has been my rock, and I constantly pull on his strength and tenacity. I can still hear him saying, "You can do this! If you work hard in the gym, your body will change!" It has no choice!" The change in my body did take place. However, not into this athletic machine I thought I envisioned for years, but into a better, stronger, leaner, faster and yes still curvy- Me! `

I am a witness that if you keep striving, you will reach your goals and discover mysteries about yourself. Mysteries of untapped strength and fortitude. You will also reveal how tenacious, courageous and smart you are. You will realize that no excuse is greater than your destiny.

I plan to make my shift by:

_____

_____

_____

_____

_____

_____

_____

_____

_____

_____

_____

_____

_____

_____

_____

_____

FITNESS
SHIFT PASS
FITNESSSHIFT.COM

"DON'T STRUGGLE WITH
EXCUSES. RISE UP AND
BATTLE FOR YOUR
HEALTH."

-Delayna K. Watkins

info@womenwellnesslounge.com

4

Shifting Through a Lifetime of Wellness

"The path to a healthy life begins where you start."
—DELAYNA K. WATKINS

In just a few hours the heavy breathing, sweat, and pain was all worth it. No, I didn't just finish a workout! I was holding an 8lb 3oz baby boy in my arms. We prepared for this day and things were coming together just as we had imagined, until it was time to leave the hospital. The journey to a mental mess began the moment I attempted to get dressed in my pre-pregnancy clothing that were so neatly packed in my overnight bag. I was in the bathroom struggling with the pink-colored pants that wouldn't budge beyond my thighs. Suddenly I became light-headed, dizzy, and everything went black in an instant. I woke up with the nurse and doctor explaining that I was found unresponsive on the bathroom floor. The severe acute anemia caused an episode of syncope (passing out), but those pink pants would send my emotions swirling out of control.

Later the next day, I arrived home with my new bundle of joy and I was physically feeling better, but mentally I was stuck on why those pink pants didn't fit like last time. Four years earlier, I went through the same scenario when I delivered my beautiful daughter except I was able to leave the hospital in the size 4 pants that I packed. Those pants slid on so easily, felt very comfortable and everyone commented that I didn't look like I was ever pregnant! Why didn't that happen this time? The answer to that question would be revealed in various ways over the next few months.

Shifting the Expectation

My expectation was derived from a previous experience, so I knew that the result was possible and could be repeated. I didn't just imagine or dream that I lost my pregnancy weight once the baby was delivered because it happened before. I became so stuck on this expectation that I began to blame the baby, my husband, and my body as the reasons I didn't experience that outcome once again. I would hold my son and think, you're so cute but you made mommy fat. Then, tell my husband that he wanted a boy and boys mess your body up during pregnancy. That negative thinking went on for about six months and the baby weight stayed in the same place. A shift in the expectation occurred during my son's 6-month baby check-up. The doctor pulled out a chart and began to compare his growth to the expected development of other 6-month olds. At that moment, I realized that I wanted to experience an outcome that wasn't designed to meet my expectation. I never considered what factors may affect the weight loss. First of all, I had gained close to 60lbs with this pregnancy and was on bedrest for the last month. Compared to the last pregnancy where I gained nearly 30lbs and was very active until I gave birth.

Developing an appropriate expectation, which is a strong belief that something will happen is an important factor in determining the outcome. It may seem silly because you know what you want and expect to happen but being clear and appropriate increases the likelihood of success. Take these three steps to successfully shift your expectation:

1. **Assess the here and now**—what is going on in your life that may impact what you expect

2. **Don't compare**—relatable information and ideas are easily embraced and can be seen as obtainable. (Ex. "If she can do it, I can too" or "I did it before and can do it again.")

3. **Address variables**—ack of time, money, or resources can impact how you develop an expectation

Shifting the Outcome

I decided at least a month before going to the hospital that I would be losing the baby weight. I thoughtfully packed that overnight back with two outfits and both were cute pre-pregnancy clothing that I was anxious to wear after 9 months. That pre-planned action set the tone for my anticipated outcome of wearing one of those outfits home from the hospital. So, for the next month I wasn't mentally preparing for or thinking about the possibility that I wouldn't return to my pre-pregnancy weight or size. Instead I allowed the clothes in that bag, my previous experience and the strong desire to lose the weight lead me on a path to outcome drama. Some version or scenario of the pink pants fiasco constantly replayed in my mind and the ending was always different than reality. In reality, I was discharged home in a size large scrub pants provided by the hospital and a pink shirt. That entire scene represented failure and disappointment to me because it was not the perfect outcome I planned. It felt more like the aftermath of a bad prank gone wrong.

Upon returning home, I refused to buy clothes in this "new size" so I continued to wear maternity clothing and the size large scrub pants until the weight disappeared! I'm not sure how I expected the weight to disappear, but I knew it didn't belong on my body. I simply kept feeling that losing the baby weight would solve all my problems and make me feel so much better. Here I go again wishing and wanting an outcome that was not clearly defined or planned appropriately. For nearly 3 months I kept trying to get those pink pants past my thighs and kept them in the drawer next to the maternity pants. This was supposed to be a motivation technique, instead it was a constant reminder of the before and after that never happened. I hit a brick wall and needed to shift my desired outcome. Take these three steps to shift your outcome:

1. **Set realistic expectations**—generalizing and keeping the expectation simple makes the outcome measurable and achievable

2. **Check your emotions**—how you feel shows up in what you expect (happy feelings want something different than sad feelings)

3. **Act accordingly**—you begin to take action and work on achieving a positive outcome when the expectation is clear and appropriate

Shifting Into Action

My son's 6-month check-up provided mental clarity and it was the last time I had a pink pants pity party. I finally realized that expecting to walk out of that hospital in those pink pants set my life on a new journey toward health and wellness. My repeated attempts to understand why history didn't repeat itself kept me in a pattern of inaction. It was like I couldn't move past the fact that I was dealing with this bad outcome. My reflection on the ridiculous expectation revealed that it was filled with emotion and came from a place of desperation. I was 8 months pregnant on bedrest, missed wearing size 4 clothes, and knew it was possible to quickly lose the baby weight. I expected this would happen without difficulty and I didn't plan to do anything else to get the results. No action meant no results and no results put me on an emotional rollercoaster.

Developing an inappropriate expectation gave me a disastrous outcome and I didn't know what to "do" about it. I became stuck in my emotions and played mental gymnastics with the situation. I found myself in a very unhealthy cycle of making poor choices. At that moment, I decided to change my expectation. With the new expectation, I was committed to making healthier choices and moving my body at least three times a week. The anticipated outcome is better emotional health, weight loss, and a lifetime of happiness. I know it sounds like a commercial, but I was able to immediately shift into action with this new plan. Take these three steps to shift into action:

1. **Begin immediately**—this helps to develop a routine and increase accountability

2. **Address potential barriers**—make a plan to overcome anything that may interfere with successfully completing an action

3. **Start with the easiest action**—gaining momentum will make the journey worth embracing

Shifting for a Lifetime of Wellness

The pink pants story developed into a movement of shifting the lifestyle of women across the globe. As a nurse, I realized that this experience was more than an individual or isolated event. The process and consequences were applicable to every woman on a larger scale beyond the pair of pants that no longer fit. I created the Total Woman Lifestyle Community which focuses on educating and encouraging women to embrace a healthier mind, body and spirit lifestyle. Women successfully nurture others with love, kindness, and care, but neglect to observe the energy for self-care. My self-care took me to the gym 4-5 times a week and I enjoyed how it made me feel. This time the heavy breathing, sweat, and pain was actually the result of a workout! It has been more than 10 years and I'm still shifting...

I plan to make my shift by:

_____

_____

_____

_____

_____

_____

_____

_____

_____

_____

_____

_____

FITNESS SHIFT PASS
FITNESSSHIFT.COM

"TAKE IT PERSONAL AND GET HEALTHY NOW."

-Dr. Brenda Bradley

info@drbtbradley.com

5

Legal Foods of Mass Destruction

"Allow food to be your medicine, not your poison"
—Dr. Brenda Bradley

It was 1982. I was fifteen and had experienced one of the worst dreams ever! I remember it as though it just happened yesterday. In this dream, I had graduated high school and moved far away from home. Several years later, I received an urgent message telling me that I must go back home. My family and friends were sick and dying. Yet, no one knew the reason why. Once I arrived back in country, I was escorted to a room and briefed about the conditions. Although no one knew the causes of sickness and death, I was given chemical protective gear to wear and a medical bag.

After the briefing I was whisked away by helicopter and dropped off in a field. I was by myself. As I walked toward the nearest city, I saw people lying in the street and in the grass. They were sick and many had died. As I continued walking trying to get to my family's house, people were pulling and grabbing at me. I promised them that I would come back as soon as I went to check on my family. When I arrived at my family's house - there were pigs, chickens, and cows in the yard and none were sick. I opened the front door and there was a note scribbled on the wall that said, "Please help us!" As I approached one of the bedrooms, I opened the door and I saw my family. It was a horrific sight! There was blood everywhere and some were unrecognizable.

This dream has stayed with me for over thirty-four years and I never really understood why. Each time this dream would appear, I always found myself crying and asking God to please explain and to help me make sense of it. Finally at the age of 48, it was revealed but only after my own personal trial and tribulation.

After fifteen years of military service, I was hit by a drunk driver. Although my injuries were not life threatening, the Air Force released me because I was no longer fit for duty and received an honorable discharge. Several years later, I found myself standing on a battle field in the midst of a vicious war I knew nothing about. I didn't have a winning chance. Not too long after leaving the military, I began to gain weight, but brushed it off. I heard that as a woman gets older her metabolism slows down; which causes her to gain weight. During this time, I had gone from a size ten to a size twelve. It bothered me because my lifestyle didn't promote or endorse this type of behavior. It was difficult to accept. Therefore, in an effort, to make sure I didn't gain any additional weight, I increased my gym visits from two to three days per week to three to four days a week.

After approximately 2 months, I was no longer a size 12, but a size 14. I was in total shock. How could this be and why was this happening? To help me combat this issue, I decided to put my pride on the shelf and joined a local weight loss center. Did I lose weight? Yes, I did....BUT, as soon as I stopped using their products and service; the weight found its way back and brought some extra pounds with it. I tried several weight loss programs and joined other companies as well. They helped but I was never satisfied. So now, I'm bigger and I am broke and could no longer afford to put my body or my bank account through this. I made a conscientious decision to keep eating healthy and to increase my gym visits again. Instead of going 3 to 4 times per week, I started going 4 to 5 times per week and sometimes twice in a day. I would go in the morning before going to work and in the evening after leaving work. Again, I didn't lose one pound. I gained and it was all fat. Now, I am no longer a size 14, I am a size 16 and 18 weighing in at 236 pounds.

One day, during an appointment, I recall my doctor telling me that I was a borderline diabetic, my blood pressure and cholesterol was high. She advised me to lose weight. I was really at my wits end. I was so lost. I really didn't know what to do. I was out of options. How could this happen to me? I had always been very active and I ate very well. I knew that it was only a matter of time before depression came knocking, but I was determined to fight this battle.

A few months later, I went to have my quarterly colonic and told my dear friend, who was also the Hydrotherapist, that something was truly wrong with me. I poured my heart out by telling her all about the things that was going on with my weight and how I was going to go to the doctor to have my thyroid checked. There had to be something wrong because there's no way a person can be so active and instead of losing, I was gaining.

I remember that day as though it was yesterday. She looked directly at me and with excitement and laughter in her voice and said, "Brenda, girl, I know exactly what you need!" It was as though a beautiful melody had just begun to play. Something deep in my soul woke up and started to do a happy dance. However, the melody came to an abrupt halt when she told me that I needed to read a book called, *The Hallelujah Diet.* So many ugly thoughts came to my mind. Oh my goodness, what are they going to think of next ~ wow! Someone had actually put the word "HALLELUJAH" in front of the word "DIET." As fate would have it, I decided to order the book. The book arrived on a Thursday. I was off on Friday, and on Saturday afternoon, I had finished reading the entire book.

This book touched my soul mentally and spiritually. Other than the bible, never before had I been so moved. I knew my life would be changed forever.

During Lent I decided to give up meat for 40 days only! I prayed hard because I knew it was going to be the hardest thing that I would ever do and I needed strength. To my surprise, I survived the entire 40 days. I had excluded all meat to include eggs, milk, and cheese. After the 40 days, I had lost 33 pounds. I couldn't believe it. I felt GREAT! I was so proud of myself and to celebrate, I treated myself to this upscale restaurant in Washington DC. I ordered grilled salmon, a baked potato, and a side salad. Remember I only gave up meat for 40 days! As soon as I took the first bite and within minutes, I felt really sick and had to leave immediately to go home. A week later my son, Brandon, came to visit and we went bowling. While at the bowling alley, Brandon ordered fries and while waiting for my turn to bowl I grabbed and ate one of his fries. Guess what? I felt really sick and had to leave immediately to go home.

The next day I called my brother, Jarvis, who was a vegetarian at the time and told him about my two ordeals. He simply laughed and said, "You're definitely a vegan. Your body will no longer accept meat." "But fries are not meat," I replied. "You are right but because the fries were cooked in the same oil as meat, your body recognized it and didn't want it," was his response. At that point, I had no idea what I was doing. However, by this time, I had lost 40 pounds and there was no way I was going back to my old eating habits which caused my health to decline. Sitting in complete silence and wondering what to do, I grabbed my laptop and googled, "What do Vegans eat?" To my surprise, a woman named Tracye McQuirter, who had been a vegan for over 25 plus years, was offering a cooking class in her home. It was during her cooking class that I began to see light at the end of the tunnel. I didn't stop there. I decided to go back to school to study nutrition and to learn more about the industry and ways I could help others.

Excessive weight and preventable illnesses are crippling our society. Our food supply is unsafe and although such foods are legal, they are causing mass destruction. According to the National Institutes of Health (NIH), in the United States alone, Americans are suffering from Cardiovascular Disease, Cancer, Diabetes, and Autoimmune Disorders. Over 80 million people are classified as obese and sadly, nearly 90 percent of our children can't pass a fitness test.

I realized that my problem wasn't the gym, it was the food. Today, we are faced with a war on legal foods that are causing mass destructions of every race. Many people are sick and dying from preventable diseases. The dream I had when I was 15 years old is today's reality.

Today I am proud to admit that I am a vegan. Through my work and passion for healthy eating and living, I answered the call to become a Certified Integrative Nutrition Health Coach. Determined to break free from the Standard American Diet which is known to do more harm than good, my goal is to inspire others to lead the charge for healthy eating and exercise. No other position has ever given me the gratification I receive from helping others. My journey back to the garden has saved my life and has opened my heart. As God continues to give me strength, I will continue to fight this battle while helping others to achieve the optimal health they were meant to have.

God Bless!

I plan to make my shift by:

_____

_____

_____

_____

_____

_____

_____

_____

_____

_____

_____

_____

_____

_____

FITNESS SHIFT PASS

FITNESSSHIFT.COM

"I AM THE NUTRITIONAL GATEKEEPER OF MY HOME. THEREFORE, I SOW SEEDS OF LIFE AND NOT DEATH. NOW, THAT'S LOVE."

Kim Griffin

kg15400@gmail.com

6

Do I Really Love My Family to Life or Death?

"We are curse breakers and history makers."
—KIM GRIFFIN

As we walk through this life we are given a responsibility by God to nourish and cherish our family. Surely, I believe that is true and I want to spend as much time as I can with my husband and my children. I hear so many sayings and quotes that talk about family being "all that we have" but I must admit that at times, I was not nourishing mine as if they were all that I had. Being a new wife that became a stay home mom was challenging for me. These new roles brought upon unanticipated stress due to me being out of balance in the midst of a huge transition. I failed at providing a healthy diet for my family several times, and I am not proud of it. In the midst of my failures, I would hear a soft voice always whispering things to me about health concerning my family and I felt a conviction knowing that I can and should do better.

As a new mom, I would meet other moms at kids events and they talked about how they loved baking and making all kinds of treats for their kids. In many of these cases, however, this became part of their identity and "treats" soon became an everyday staple in their family's diet which resulted in weight gain for the mom's and their families. What made me feel uncomfortable is that the majority of these moms never mentioned getting their bodies back in shape. Their identity, who they were before they started having kids, started to be lost. As a matter of fact, it is fair to say that they were comfortable still looking like they were expecting. As for me, I looked the same way, overweight and feeling overwhelmed but my weight gain came from stress and eating the kid's food. As I consumed food I knew I should not be eating, God would whisper "Kim what are you doing, you have a health ministry inside of you for you and your lineage". I knew deep down in the inside, something had to change because I was uncomfortable in a size 14 and got sick of secretly unbuttoning my pants before I sat down.

There were times early in my marriage while sitting at the Thanksgiving table with my in-laws and my family, God would start asking me questions:

"Are you hungry, or are you bored?"

"Why are you sleepy. What did you just eat?"

"You just ate one hour ago, why are you eating again?"

I would answer honestly, "I am eating again because this food is good, I have never had mac and cheese with cream cheese in it before, on top of that if I do not eat more they may think I'm being rude."

Then I would hear God's voice louder saying "You are a chosen generation, you are different, and life and death is in the power of the tongue".

Eventually I gave in to the urging of God because apparently He was not going to leave me alone. It was up to me to shift my mindset and act upon creating a healthy new tradition. I educated myself and took action, incorporating more than just the yearly Daniel fast into my family's diet. I started taming my tongue and telling myself to do better. I cleaned out my pantry, found healthier options, created and became a part of a healthier community and made conscious, intentional steps daily to change my habits. These daily steps eventually became who I am.

Within a three year time frame, even my in-laws became more health conscience and accepted my gifts. I must tell you it was not easy. My mother in-law is a great strong woman who gave me problems with trying to introduce healthy options to the family. I remember one transparent talk we had about what the meaning of food was and how it related to family. She said "I was taught that food was an expression of love and I regret some things". I appreciated that understanding because that is something I could learn from and create healthier expressions of love within and outside of food. I had to take some bold stances in my house because my husband is the baby boy of his family and he was used to having his favorite meals. As I prayed to God to allow his tongue to desire fruits and veggies, the scripture I stood on was "A wise woman builds her house and fools plucks it downs with her own hands". I knew that if I continued to buy the food and make it, regardless if he ate it, he would give in. And needless to say, he did after a few years and he now looks younger and his energy is off the charts. He thanks me and tells me "You saved my life. My bad sinuses I would get yearly are now gone". It is in my hands to improve the quality of his life.

We often walk through life thinking that what we eat will never affect us. However, there are plenty of studies and evidence that say the opposite. My brother Rodney dropped dead of a heart attack in June of 2016 at my cousin's restaurant. My cousin was proud to announce at his funeral that he gave my brother his last meal. Let me tell you, the meal was for my brother who neglected his hypertension: it was a 2 piece dark meat fried chicken dinner with fries. I think what my cousin was really proud of was that my brother passed to glory in the midst of family and he was there. Approximately two years prior to his passing my brother was hospitalized due to a mild stroke which bothered me to my core. My husband agreed with me that Rodney needed to stay with us for a couple of months, and in that time, I loved on him with some good healthy food. After staying with us, Rodney left from my home 60 pounds lighter with better eating habits. His supervisor told me after he passed " Rodney had never looked as good as he did once he left your home". When I have quiet moments and think of that time, God whispers to me " Well done, now that's love." My husband told me that "your love helped extend his time on earth" so when I grieve and mourn, I can also rejoice.

Family is all that we have and gathering together is priceless. When I think of traditions it usually starts with oldest southern woman of the family affectionately known as "Big Mama". Her wisdom is so deep and profound that you would find it useful in your life. Unfortunately, " Big Mama's" are not known for wisdom but for scrumptious southern recipes. And "Big Mama" has to take her insulin that is in a little clear container in the refrigerator with a needle that she must inject into her arm. I remember growing up thinking that was normal and nothing was wrong with it. Don't you think it's time for a "Little Mama" or a "Little Nana" to step up on the scene and redirect her lineage for a long healthy life? What is going to your name? Big Mama, Big Nana or even Big Poppy? You know the title. Let's be curse breakers and history makers in our families. It starts by loving our families to life in the kitchen.

Has your mind shifted?

Love Testimonies:

My daughter: After changing her diet, the chronic eczema on her body went away.

My husband: His almost guaranteed twice a year sinus infections no longer occur. He rarely gets sick, lost 20 pounds and at 40 has the same waist line as he did as a senior in high school playing football.

Close friend's daughter: She would constantly disturb her class with uncontrollable behaviors. Once identifying the problem within her diet, she became a focused, attentive student.

This chapter is dedicated to my loving brother Rodney Williams, I am looking forward to breaking some good bread together with you one day in heaven. To God be the glory.

I plan to make my shift by:

_____

_____

_____

_____

_____

_____

_____

_____

_____

_____

_____

_____

_____

_____

7

Fit For the Shift

"It's one thing to know what to do.
It's another to actually do it."
—Maricia Sherman

As I sat nervously in my seat listening at the event hostess read my bio, I began to feel the tear ducts opening in my eyes. Was she really reading about me? Had I really accomplished writing a book, earning my master's degree, starting my own business, becoming an ordained minister? This poor southern girl, who grew up in a little trailer with no running water, was approaching the podium shaking in her boots, but I was ready! As I placed my notes gently on the side, I reminded myself to breathe easy and remember to make the most of every opportunity. It was my moment to let the world hear my significant voice, my customized ringtone. I took a deep breath and remembered all the sacrifices that have been made for this moment. I confidently stood tall, look out into the packed audience, and simply said, "Good Morning, my name is Fit for the Shift!"

Of course, I did not always feel "fit for the shift." This thing called life has a way of spinning out of control if you let it. Which is exactly what I had done on several occasions. Due to many misguided choices, I found myself aimlessly wandering around, physically, mentally, and emotionally depleted. I was constantly asking myself, "Girl, when are you going to stop dreading life?" As humans, we all too often forget that what we have been given so beautifully wrapped in the form of life is a marvelous gift. Not only is it a gift, but it has added characters that bring incredible value. Characters such as family, friends, and wonderful associates. It is only when we begin to devalue the process and journey that we find ourselves in compromising positions. It is then that we either slip into mediocrity or we decide to pick up the pace. For me, picking up the pace was way overdue. I mean, it had been a long time since I took that dreadful drive to my mother's house literally sobbing the entire way and although life had drastically changed for the better since that drive, in my mind, it seemed just like yesterday. What a sight I must have been!

Driving with 3 small children from New York City to Mississippi is tough enough but when you have a million thoughts running around in your head, it was insanity. I was not even sure how I was seeing the highway through my blind anger. Actually, it was rage. But to whom should I direct the rage? It was clear that I had contributed to this insane unfolding scene but did I really deserve this? I was now facing the very real fact of a pending divorce, single parenthood, and the uncomfortable nagging question of, "Will I ever love again?" Should I turn around and return? I had to make a decision. This rollercoaster ride was not fun. It had become bumpy and dangerous. I had to come to grips with where my life was taking me. My indecisiveness was affecting my whole life. Mostly, my children. I can still hear that piercing sound of my oldest daughter asking that infamous question, "Mommy, why are we sitting in the parking lot?" Turning around to the backseat, I would look into the face of such innocence and for the first time realize not only am I sitting in this dark and rainy Walmart parking lot at 2AM but she and her siblings are sitting here as well. My chaotic decisions were affecting them too! Why had I forgotten that? My selfishness had placed my life on a slippery slope by which they were drifting down with me. Her question would shift my determination from that moment forward. So with tears streaming down my face, I jumped out of that van, ran to the pay phone, in the pouring rain I might I add, and dialed an old familiar number. Soaking wet from head to toe, I apprehensively said, "Mom, I need to come home." Unknowingly, I had just made a step toward becoming "fit for the shift."

As the weeks went by at my mother's, I made some difficult decisions in my attempt to move forward. I had arrived at her home two days after that rainy night in the parking lot, broken, hungry, and in despair. Thankfully progress was being made and here I was a couple of months later hopefully about to receive one of the greatest breakthroughs of my life. Would they accept me into the program? Please God say yes! I really needed to hear some good news. I was becoming frustrated and even more discouraged. The embarrassment alone from the never ending questions of relatives was enough to send a person into a panic mode. It was like my separation and divorce was the hot topic of the community. Plus, I certainly was delirious from lack of sleep and worry. Not to mention, I had been cut off from any finances connected to my marriage. I was wrapping pennies to purchase diapers, spending two dollars on gas, and had begun only buying beans and bologna to eat. I was desperate for a new start. This phone call had better bring me fortune. So with a cracked voice, I pushed the answer button on that old beat up cordless phone and whispered, "Hello". Unknowingly, with that tiny "hello", I was becoming "fit for the shift."

Walking into that classroom, I couldn't believe that it was all happening. The director had called and said that I had been accepted into the program! Elated, I had begun preparing my mind to mentally embrace myself for what was ahead. Being in college and raising 3 young daughters would not be an easy feat. But I had prayed and I believed. I looked down at the introduction sheet, wrote my name under incoming student, and silently declared that I was capable of accomplishing all that I put my hands too. Sliding into my seat, a back one, I stared at the syllabus and began to pray. "Please Lord, give me the ability to understand. I have undertaken so many transitions in the last year. It all seems to be a dream filled with many ups and downs, twists and turns, and everything else in between. But I acknowledge you in all my ways. Thank you for calming the uncertainties about my readiness, my stability, and my God given ability and more. So Lord, thank you for a second chance." Filled with unexpected happiness, I knew I was awakening from any illusions and was creating a better reality. I was becoming "fit for the shift."

Hopefully, by now, you have chimed in on what the message of my heart is to you the reader. In each scenario, I had to realize that I must be healthy in my mind, body, and spirit before I could ever begin shifting into a new season. I had to understand that happiness and peace were never meant to be illusions. That they could actually be attained and enjoyed in reality. But only when I began becoming "fit for the shift" did I begin to see that it was possible to live a life of fulfillment. You see, we are all excited when a shift takes place but the truth of the matter is that we must prepare to be "fit" for it. Mental and emotional fitness is just as important as physical fitness. How many of us know people who have it going on as it relates to the exterior appearance but are seemingly miserable within? It is because somewhere along the lines that person did not become fit in their mind and heart. They entered into a life season without first being sure if their mindset was healthy enough to sustain the season. Entering into a new shift without properly laying to rest sleeping giants that we have awakened will only cause us to abort the impending shift's process. We must prepare and we must acknowledge any pretenses that would keep us from becoming, "fit for the shift."

You see each step I took during those life transitions, I asked God to prepare me for the next. I asked him to not allow any shifts to take place until I had healed, come to grips with, and acknowledged pain or disappointment from the last shift. For instance, although I was shaking in my boots when I arrived to class as a new student that morning, I knew that I had to press forward. I had to actually walk through the door, sit in the chair, and acknowledge that I was a single mom in college with 3 small children. I questioned whether I would be able to keep up, if I would understand the class material, and furthermore, if I could financially maintain. I was going to have to operate out of total and pure faith. I had to release my limited mind. I had to make a resolution to not quit. When my wonderful husband first asked me out, I said no. I knew I was not ready for that shift. It was some time before I was only able to firmly believe I had become fit for a particular shift. I had done this by successfully navigating through the previous life shift. My mind was not toggled with bitterness, anger, or regret. I had acknowledged that my abusive childhood had pushed me into misguided relationships and I had received counseling. All those steps allowed me to become "fit" for my next shift. My aim is to present this message so that you are geared up and ready to make that move as well. Your next move will be the calculated strategic warfare designed to fight the enemies of your soul. It will be designed to fight negative mindsets whether it is that of your own or another's. Are you ready to become "fit for the shift?" I believe it's time.

It is time to make that move. I did not say the move or a move; I said THAT move. I want to speak to that move that scares you every time you think on it. The move that keeps you up at night dreaming and you feel is unattainable. The move that you know could alter your life forever in a positive manner. Are you ready to intensify your groove? To become fit for your shift? I believe your answer is yes! With that being so, let's make preparation for success. Dr. Martin Luther King, Jr. states "We are now faced with the fact that tomorrow is today. We are confronted with the fierce urgency of now." You see, our "now" is upon us. It is time for a fitness shift, concerning not only our body, but mind and soul. Let's become fit for the shift by identifying areas that need attention. Let's become fit for the shift by closing doors, adjusting our circle, making amends. Do not enter the shift with the same condemning ways that become a habitual cycle. Enter into that shift being fit to handle what is next. Enter into it by being aggressively confident that you are capable, that you are uniquely designed and equipped for your next life assignment, on whatever level that may be on. Become "fit for the shift" through discipline, humbleness, the power of love, and a sound mind. Keep your head up and your confidence strong. Within you lies the ability to escalate your desires into tangibles. The nights may seem long, fear may knock at your door, but inside of you rages the strength to overcome every obstacle lying in your path. Do not allow yourself to sit in the parking lot of life. Get out of that parking lot and rage on. I finally realized that moment in that parking lot so many years ago was carving me, shaping and molding me. I am now "buff and cut" with potential. And so are you! It's your turn. Your life is waiting. Your greatness is waiting and I am assured that you will be able to look into the face of the shift and say, "Hello Shift, I am fit for you."

I plan to make my shift by:

_____

_____

_____

_____

_____

_____

FITNESS
SHIFT PASS
FITNESSSHIFT.COM

"WHEN YOU ARRIVE TO YOUR DESTINATION, RE-MEMBER IT IS NOT YOUR FINAL STOP. CONTINUE STRETCHING YOURSELF."

-Regina Robinson

info@reginarobinsonspeaks.com

8

My Life Weighed More Than My Skirt Size

"It wasn't about the outer weight weighing me down; it was the inner weight I was carrying that weighed me down."
—REGINA ROBINSON

First, giving God the honor, glory and praise for allowing me to share my story of how He moved me from triumph to victory. I know what it is like to not have someone encouraging you. There was a time when I would wake up going from day to day with my eyes open, but the darkness of my failures, fears, doubt and lack of confidence haunted my every move. I was depressed, unhappy, and broken on the inside; however I had learned to mask my pain so well you would have never known.

One day, I asked myself the hardest question in my life: "Will you remain entrenched in darkness or will you walk in God's light?" For the first time, I acknowledged to myself that I was broken. I got down on my knees to have an intimate talk and cry with God. It was the ugliest cry I had ever had. Why? Because I was determined that when I arise, my heart, mind, and spirit would be RELEASED from the deep dark hole I had built for myself.

Everything changed for me that day; I stopped looking in the mirror at the broken woman who I would tell daily, *You are Ugly,*

Unhappy, and FAT. In fact you look like you're four months pregnant and we both know you are not. God shared a shocking word with me during my ugly cry. He said, "My daughter you are indeed pregnant." For so long I had refused to give birth to my past hurts, failures, disappointments, shame, and so much more. God shared with me; "Until you're ready to expose and bare all, you will remain pregnant." That was my revelation. I realized it was not about the outer weight wearing me down it was the inner weight I was carrying that weighed me down. You see, I finally realized "My Life Weighed More Than My Skirt Size."

I remember growing up playing the game of "Double Dutch" outside with my friends. Everyone thought they were the best jumper on the playground. I was no different. When it was my turn, I would bounce back and forth outside the rope until I felt the turn was PERFECT for me.

I carried that same Double Dutch effect through life; bouncing as if I was still that great jumper. However, somewhere along my journey I lost my confidence of when to jump in. Instead of courageously jumping in, I bounced back and forth through life weighed down by my past imperfections and insecurities of not feeling worthy or good enough. I was bouncing through life, lying to myself and everyone else. When people would ask how I was doing I would say, "I am blessed and highly favored." How many of you know you can mask your pain with others, but when you look in the mirror it will reveal your true reflection?

Unhappy with my reflection, I went on a two year journey of self-discovery to determine what was causing the foundation of my life to weaken. I was immediately reminded of the anchor that holds my life together and that is the word of God. A scripture that dropped in my spirit was Luke 7:36-38, the story of the woman with the alabaster jar. She too was a woman who had suffered from past sin in her life just as I had. Can you take a minute and imagine with me the power she felt as she entered the room with Jesus? I was reminded of all the pain I had encountered {hurt, disappointment, failure, insecurity...and so much more} but at that very moment I knew none of that mattered. Why? I knew God had the power to wash everything away and restore the confidence within me I had lost along the way.

CeCe Winans said it best: "Don't be angry when you see me wash His feet with my tears and dry them with my hair. You weren't there the night Jesus found me. You did not feel what I felt when He wrapped His loving arms around me. You don't know the cost of my oil." I stopped waiting on God, realizing He was always present; in fact He was waiting on me.

I realized the inner weight I was carrying began to weigh me down on the outside. When I would look in the mirror instead of telling myself you are beautiful, I would say to myself daily, "you are FAT." I was ashamed to look at myself in the mirror. What I saw on the outside was a reflection of what I felt on the inside. I was still carrying the shame from past burdens and baggage of failed relationships. Food became the steroid to ease my addiction of the continuous pain I felt. I realized sixty pounds heavier that no matter how much I believed food was relieving the pain (depression, sleepless nights, crying, and shame) it was in fact causing me more pain.

The power of my weight relied on the gravity of my willingness to shift my mindset. I could not keep doing the same things expecting different results. I woke up one morning, looked in the mirror, and decided enough was enough. I knew my journey would require me to think differently. If not, I would lose the weight on the outside, but in my heart, mind, and spirit I would still be FAT. So, I stopped hiding from my challenges and acknowledged they were necessary in order to get to my destination. When I faced the truth about my internal weight, God anchored my commitment and released the external weight.

I could have gone to any gym and worked out, but I knew the ROOT that anchored my weight was tied to more than just a dumb bell, treadmill or stair stepper. In fact, it was a direct result of my FEAR to face the truth. On the inside, I was playing tug of war with the woman I was and the woman I wanted to become.

I had to acknowledge that in order to arrive at my destination it would require my willingness to take the journey and stay the course despite the struggles and setbacks I would encounter. Now you remember me saying I woke up and said, "enough was enough." However, that is often easier said then done. You must be willing to take action. So I did!

I got on the phone and called, *Candice The Wellologist* and said, "I need you." Her response was, "Chic just show up." When I hung up, I immediately allowed the negative internal dialogue – what I call head trash – to intervene. As we often do, I began to entertain the negative questions: *Girl what are you doing? Are you really ready? Can you really lose the weight?* I began to doubt the decision I made in my heart, mind and spirit.

I had to remind myself it was not ok to entertain negative conversations with myself, especially if I did not plan on winning. Well, of course I am competitive by nature, so I had no intentions of losing. I made the decision to workout with *Candice The Wellologist* twice a week. As much as I dreaded working out I would show up wining and crying about the workout. Candice would just say, "It's ok just whine while you pedal, lift, and jump." She would say remember, "Nothing will change unless you change. You have to push past this; you get to decide." I began to realize the potential of my greatness was tied up in my willingness to push past the sweat and tears. On days it got tough I did not bail out instead I put in the time and work to become the best version of ME.

As I started to lose weight (size 16 to 10) people would tug on my clothes and say, "Girl you are so skinny you think you cute" – that made me feel some kind of way. I asked myself; "Wow! Was I really that big?" Did my weight really show? See what they couldn't see was that my battle stemmed far beyond the outer weight they could see – they missed it – it was the inner weight I carried (depression/unhappy/didn't love myself/didn't believe I was worthy) that weighed my life down like a ton of bricks. If they only knew that when I looked in the mirror every day, I was unhappy with the reflection I saw on the inside. They could only see the outside FAT I purged which was an added bonus. The true blessing was the day I surrendered and allowed God to build up the broken woman and restore me to become the woman of God, He destined me to be.

Today you are reading about a woman who God has made whole with His touch. God touched my inner most soul and restored all the broken pieces that were: Shattered *yet not broken*—Glory to God! I now know my scars and bruises are a testament that God could use even me. I no longer judge myself based on my past hurts, failures, and disappointments. I realized that everything I went through was necessary. God was preparing me for greater.

That is why today I no longer keep score of what I did in the past; instead I hit the reset button on my life. I stopped standing in my brokenness. In fact, I am grateful I took the jump in expectation of the great things God has in store for my life. As I walk in my purpose, I no longer live in my story instead I stand on my story. Every chance I get, I remind people that it is not because of me but surely it is His grace and mercy that my light shines brightly today as I show up in my power.

Forgive me for my excitement; "That my life no longer weighs more than my skirt size"!!! With God's presence, I discovered a newfound peace, joy, and love. Today I fearlessly strut in my confidence without apology.

GOD THANK YOU FOR ACCEPTING ME!

Regina Robinson
Inner Confidence Strategist
ReginaRSpeaks
www.reginarobinsonspeaks.com

I plan to make my shift by:

9

Investing Into My Greatest Asset-Me

"There is grace to empower you to be
all that destiny requires of you."
—ROCHELLE MALONE

What do you do when life pulls the rug from under you? I found out for myself in 2007. You get a wake-up call as to who you really are as a person and what you are made of. As a certified personal development and resiliency coach, I came face to face with the reality that I really did not know who I was as a person. I had lost "me" in the process of living life. Life has a way of getting your attention and my life certainly gained my attention while causing me to make changes; one being a fitness shift that catapulted me to the next era of my life.

2007 started out as a wonderful year for me and my family; it was the year we were finally beginning the see the fruit of our labor in ministry. My husband and I met in college and were college sweethearts. Ministry was his passion and I loved God, but had no clue about ministry. We were married in my senior year of college and his first year of graduate school. We wanted to get married young so we could devote ourselves to serving God through ministry. We set our heart and minds to grow in ministry to not just be efficient, but also effective in ministry; and as our church grew so did our family to include four beautiful girls. It was our joy to serve God and our community while offering hope and encouragement through biblical teaching as well as leadership training and development. My husband and I had sacrificed and invested so much of our time, energy and prayers into building other's lives. It was a rewarding experience to see so many people flourish and grow spiritually, personally and professionally. We were beginning to see the fruit of the seeds of faith that was planted in so many lives. We started the ministry in August 1990 with 2 others couples, a total of 6 of us, but my husband was the visionary and senior pastor. In 2007, that number of 6 members had expanded to 1500+ membership, a weekly T.V. broadcast, and annual city-wide conferences and workshops. We were making a positive impact on many people's lives.

I was living the all-American dream; I was married with four beautiful girls and co-pastoring a thriving ministry with my husband of over 17 years and fulfilling my God-given purpose, life was good! Well, I thought it was good. That is until, I was blindsided by a divorce that impacted me on multiple levels. We were working through some martial issues and I thought we were on the road to full recovery but as I soon found out, apparently not. I was raised in the south and family and church were highly esteemed. My world was my family and church and in a matter of days my world was rocked to the core. The closest image of what I experienced is the devastation and sudden destruction that happened during Hurricane Katrina, except this devastation came in a way that I had no time to prepare for it. I've heard of divorce being described as a ripping apart of two lives, regardless of how clean you try to tear it; there's still a rip in your soul. As a result of the divorce, I was literally disillusioned, and broken. I put my faith and trust in people more than I did in God and paid dearly for that choice.

I cannot stress enough of how my life revolved around my husband, family and ministry. It's hard enough to go through a divorce, even a civil divorce is hard but to have my character assassinated and my role as a mother discredited in the course of the divorce was unfathomable. The truth of the matter is, I was in a very controlling and manipulative marriage in which my love was used against me, putting me in a very unfavorable position.

I learned through trained therapists that abuse is not easily identified with the casual eye. I was aware of physical abuse, but other not so obvious forms of abuse like emotional and financial abuse were not on my radar. Emotional abuse has a way of creating an unsure footing for the person being abused. It never allows the person to feel whole or complete without the other person. "Emotional abuse is designed to chip away at a person's self-esteem, self-worth, and independence and even make them believe that without the abuser they have nothing" (Tracy, 2012). Financial abuse serves to render the victim financially powerless.

Abuse in any form makes any kind of relationship toxic. Period.

In the midst of my life spiraling out of control, I remember waking up in a panic as if I was trying to catch my breath from a nightmare. The sad truth was that I was not waking up from a nightmare, I was waking up to a nightmare! How could my life take such a crazy turn? Everything I had worked to build: my family, the ministry, and who I thought I was as a person, was gone in a matter of days. I had hit rock bottom. It did not matter how my life had gotten to this point. Quite frankly, I had no idea what I was going to do in order to get my life back.

I remember a call from Vickie and Jeffrey, my sister and my brother-in-law. Vickie, my sister, was calling to encourage me, but before she got off the phone my brother-in-law asked me a question. "Rochelle, are you working out?" he said. In that moment, I kind of thought it was an odd question, especially in the midst of all the chaos. Working out, of all things, was not on my To Do list. Regardless, Jeffrey, told me I should start working out and that it would help me during this trying time.

I thought it over, I took his advice and called my friend Belinda, these were the days before CoachBFit, and although she was not actively training, she referred me to one of her fitness trainers. With just two phone calls my fitness shift began!

Faith, prayer and fitness became my tools for this unsettling period of my life. Faith was my foundation, prayer was my spiritual outlet, and exercise became my physical outlet. I realized that I had given all of "me" away. I had to learn how to give without giving away what made me my authentic self. Fitness became that special time to focus on my greatest asset-me.

My fitness shift was about gaining mental focus during a very blurry time in my life. An intense workout prevented me from thinking or focusing on anything else other than completing my reps or a boot camp. I traded depression (anger turned inward) in exchange for exhilarating exercise to boost and release endorphins (the happy triggers of life; stress reducers), and chase sadness away.

I learned the power of choice. One of my favorite quotes is from Jim Rohn, "You can have the pain of regret or the pain of discipline". This quote spoke to me, especially regarding the responsibility I have for my health. I can discipline myself through proper diet and exercise, or I can wait for doctors to restrict my diet and require weekly exercise due to unfavorable health conditions.

My fitness shift also gave me the ability to tap into the grace of resolve and strength. There is a popular saying, "Rome wasn't built in a day". Working out and seeing physical changes is a constant process. I remember the excitement of seeing muscle definition in my arms. They weren't Angela Basset arms, but they had a little definition and I was proud of my efforts. I used the physical challenge to motivate me mentally to stay in the good fight of faith. When I am working out, I sometimes feel like I can't complete one more rep but when I push through the burn, the strength comes. This is an example of how when faced with challenging situations in life, pushing through by faith reinforces my spiritual strength which causes spiritual growth. Fitness has now become a conscious choice. I monitor what I eat, I try to exercise three to five times a week. It isn't easy but my physical and mental health are too great a price to pay otherwise.

As a personal development coach, I now look back on my situation and realize that I utilized a self-awareness technique that was introduced to me through my coach training. It's called "TTR- Self-Awareness Test". TTR represents (T)rigger= the event, conversation, or challenge that caused the stressor or problem; (T)houghts= what you say to yourself in the heat of the moment; and (R)eactions=the emotions and actions that follow. My (T)rigger was my divorce. My (T)houghts focused on my way out of my situation instead of staying too long in negative emotions. Lastly, the (R)eaction that followed was my fitness shift. This led to gaining greater mental focus and clarity through exercise, learning the power to choose and realizing that it is up to me to decide to take control of my health, both physically and mentally, as well as embracing the grace of resiliency and strength to overcome my obstacle.

The first step is a step of faith but soon grace catches up with you and helps strengthen you to overcome. Through my trying experience, I really did learn that there is only one of me and I can allow myself to be pulled in a myriad of directions but it is up to me to set healthy boundaries in my life and choose to value myself and invest in nurturing my spirit, body and soul. After all, I am my greatest asset.

References

Tracy, N. (212, July 24). *Dynamics of Emotional Abuse in Relationships, Marriage.* Retrieved August 28, 2016, from www.healthyplace.com,http://www.healthyplace.com/abuse/emotional-psychological-abuse-definitions-signs-symtoms-example/

I plan to make my shift by:

_____

_____

_____

_____

_____

_____

_____

_____

_____

_____

_____

@TIERRADESTINYREID

FITNESS SHIFT **PASS**

FITNESSSHIFT.COM

"ONCE YOU HAVE PLOWED YOUR OWN GARDEN, THE BEST THING YOU CAN DO IS PASS ON THE TOOLS TO SOMEONE WHO IS READY TO PLOW THEIR OWN."

-Tierra Destiny Reid

inquiries@tierradestinyreid.com

10

A New View Requires a New Decision

*"The release you've been waiting for is also waiting for you.
Make a conscious choice to clear your schedule and
become your own project."*
—TDR

As I sit here typing these very words on this page, I am reminded of the power of a new decision. For the past 11 years, I have struggled with my weight. After giving birth to my first child, I remained in a place of comfortable discomfort. Yup. Comfortable with settling with the disturbing truth of wishing I had the discipline to get healthy and get fit.

Prior to that, I had the perfect shape. I had always lived life as the girl that was fit and could wear anything she desired. Fashion was and still is a huge form of expression for me. So what happens when the things you desire are no longer available in your size? When your husband no longer looks at you the same? When you can barely bend over to tie your own shoes? You decide to lose the weight and get your life back. Right? Well, sort of. Deciding to do it in your mind is a lot easier than the daily action required to support the desire.

I would soon realize my biggest obstacles to date…Discipline. Will Power. Consistency. The traits that I used to be strong in when it came to business and every other goal in my life, became what felt like the battle of a lifetime.

I finally had to admit that I had a very deep relationship with food. It was my comfort. It was my safe place. It was my happy space and it was my sad space. I could toast to a celebration and then throw in as much cake as I could; or I could end a stressful day in pure delight over a box of shrimp fried rice, two egg rolls, and braised wings.

That was normal for me. ALL. THE. TIME.

I have tried to lose weight for the last 11 years and I have always wanted to deep down in my core. When people say you will do it when you want it bad enough, I get so pissed off, because you can't say what a person does not want. Many times it is tied to a lot of other factors that we tend to ignore. I was in a stressful corporate environment after having my child. I was a military spouse which meant that stability for us was more financial that physical, and there was a lot of pain deep inside of me that was a lot easier to ignore than it took to do the work.

Interestingly enough, my journey reached an all-time high in 2012. That is when I exceeded my first six figures as a retail store owner, became a national speaker, and began hosting my own empowerment conferences for women. It was great. It felt great and it was definitely my calling. However, I felt that I was flying with a broken wing.

It was time to pause and begin making new decisions. Over the course of what turned out to be a three-year journey of self-discovery and healing, Oprah Winfrey connected with me on Twitter and I was blessed to attend a private lunch with her and other OWN Ambassadors in Los Angeles. When I look at the pictures, I see the joy and the sadness at the same time. I had so many moments in which I wanted to look as amazing as the moment represented for me, but yet, I could not fit what I really wanted. I was uncomfortable and frustrated with wearing body shapers, and I had become a pro at hiding myself in photos.

After that trip, I sold my store, pulled away from everything and paused. I wanted to become clear. I wanted to dig deep and face the emotions that had been lying dormant for so long. After months of journaling, I realized that everything I was feeling and experiencing could help other women. My first book was born out of this pain, "The Power of Peace in a Pause". I began counseling and having honest conversations with people in my past. I began admitting that my marriage was very unhealthy and had probably been over for years.

It was hard to admit that food had become my choice as a comforter or friend that was always an easy swipe away. OMG. It seemed like I craved certain foods with certain emotions. It was not until I started to meet new friends who would educate me bit by bit on the different options and tips that helped them transform that I started to get results.

It seemed as though all the tips that I had gathered over the last 11 years started to come together for me, the more I healed and broke off other unhealthy interactions in my life. I started to choose myself and made a decision to honor my temple. While pregnant, I reached 242 pounds as a 5-foot woman. I eventually leveled out around 200-209. Whenever I would get serious and lose weight, I would hit the 10-pound mark and then guess what, my lack of preparation and lack of discipline would get me every time. Travel, cruises, parties, you name it…It was always a reason to "cheat" this one time.

About three months ago, I was 209. Today, I am 179. I am on my way. Hopefully by the time this book hits your hands, I will be even healthier. It is truly a daily decision each and every time you decide to eat or be active while choosing the new you over the old you. At least for me, choosing to focus on the woman who deserves to experience life freely and healthy on this earth, has allowed me to keep going this time.

A new view requires a new decision. It is so true. I don't ever judge people because it is so easy to slip back. Until we form solid new habits with a solid circle of support and tools, we are not truly setting ourselves up for success. Instead of beating myself up, I have started to cheer myself on for getting back up each time I fell off and being patient with my process. It feels good to choose to keep going. I started to realize that the emotions caused by external situations and people, is really not worth me remaining in a place less than I deserve and desire. So here's to all the people out there who have decided to choose YOU! I've learned that once we can choose ourselves with apology or shame, we can become our own project and inspire those around us to do the same.

Keep me lifted and I will do the same for you.

Love, TDR

I plan to make my shift by:

_____

_____

_____

_____

_____

_____

_____

FITNESS
SHIFT PASS
FITNESSSHIFT.COM

"I STOPPED
COMPARING MYSELF
TO OTHER QUEENS AND
JUST BECAME THE BEST
QUEEN I AM."

–Shameka Austin

shamekasinegal@yahoo.com

11

Rescued from the Mindset of Egypt

*"God gave every Queen a purpose.
Now it is time to live in it!"*
—SHAMEKA AUSTIN

I was not always in bondage. At one point in my life, I smiled just because I was alive. Then slowly it was taken away. But, let me tell you a little about my life before it went into a spiral. My father was in the Air Force and being gone a good bit of time, my mother was there to take care of home with 5 kids. My mother is the type of woman that I call antique. I could only wish to be half of the woman she is, one day. My mother would cook breakfast, lunch, and dinner. She would also have specific days to do certain chores. She made sure we were on a very tight schedule and made sure that we followed it, that way it flowed smoothly. As I grew, my father and mother wanted to protect me from pain of the world so they always decided what was best for me. My mother always made the decisions for me so there was no need for me to make decisions and I did not realize how that would cripple me later in life.

We need to teach our children to make decisions on their own , being very confident in their decision because that is how you build leaders!

In high school, I was a little different from kids my age. I was always taller and always weighed more than other teens. Leaving high school, I weighed 235 pounds not knowing that number would slowly start to grow even more. I was very active in basketball and would work hard even though every pound would nibble away at my knees with every step. I looked at my teammates and would silently wish I could magically take off the weight and create the womanly shape they were growing into. Food became an addiction. I was living to eat instead of just eating enough to live.

I was addicted and just could not pull away because I needed it to survive. Since I found a lot of happiness in food, I did not invest in friendships and defiantly did not have boyfriends so when I would talk to a guy that really liked me, I would cling quick and hard. Then I met a man, having abandonment issues, he wanted the opportunity to have a family again because his first marriage had failed. So we became enablers to each other. I wanted to be with him no matter what ,even if I saw the signs in him that said stay away! We married within 8 months of meeting and I thought life would take off and we would build an amazing empire together. Then without warning, it changed!

Private pain, public pulpit!

I looked up at his face with tears pouring from my eyes, as he was holding me down on the floor by my wrist there was a unreachable deepness in his eyes. I shook my head from side to side as he screamed at me, to escape the volume of spit coming out his mouth with no avail. Struggling, trying to get up because my baby girl, was sitting on the floor crying and my sons were looking at me through the doorway with helplessness overtaking them. My oldest son 6 years old at the time, runs and jumps on his father trying to hit him to get him off of me and then he is tossed aside. "GOD PLEASE!", I cried! All of this was because I heard a woman's voice on my voicemail saying, "Your baby needed diapers and wipes!" Yes.....

you heard right! The man who I called MY husband, had a baby with another woman! According to him, the reason he had an affair was because the other woman would tell him that, me, as the wife, did not know how to treat a real man and all she wanted to do was take care of him! That was what he longed for. What I was doing was not enough! I worked a full time job, over night, would come home, with him still in the bed, get my kids ready for school, go drop them off to school, try to sleep when my baby was resting. Then, go pick the kids up from school as well as trying to cook in between everything else that was going on. Then start all over again, back to work!! In so many words he said, He wanted somebody who cared about how they looked and did not wear bags for dresses. My weight was always an issue between us. He was very vocal about how I disgusted him when I would overeat, but I had no guidance on how to become healthier. This was not how my life was suppose to be. God, I am the Bishops daughter, a praise and worship leader and my life was not supposed to be this way! What would people say about me if they knew what was going on in my life. I minister to people every Sunday and cannot reach my own, the one who I believe to be the love of my life. He was my world. I loved him with every inch of my soul. Not remembering what I was taught as a young girl, *"Do not worship any other god, for the Lord, Who's name is Jealous, is a jealous God"*(Exodus 34:14). More food would help bury this pain. I had been so successful in building this woman that I wanted people to see. I was a PK (Preachers Kid), I knew when to lift my hands, when to praise, shout and would always put a smile on and no one knew that it was the total opposite behind my door! The fighting ceased when he felt he had got his point across. When morning came, he was sure to come meet me as I was curled up on the sofa holding my babies and my eyes swollen from every tear that fell from my face, pulling me by the hand with a soft look in his face as to tell me to come to the bedroom with him. I still did 't have the strength to leave. Why didn't I have the strength? I started to become very bitter and mean, which was the total opposite of what I was growing up. So how did I end up here, you ask? I lost GOD as my focus!

God gave every Queen a purpose and now it was time for me to live in it! I did not like who I had become. I did not like the woman I saw in the mirror. I felt disgusting and ashamed. It is a miserable feeling to not love the person you see in the mirror every morning, but God would soon change my outlook. I began to shift my mindset from being bound by depression, my weight and by the obstacles that I thought I would never overcome! I now had pull my mask off and put my crown on! Church had become the place where I had peace and I did not have to argue with anyone. I said church because I had completely left my first love and that was Jesus Christ! During my darkest times, I was not looking for Him to be my comforter, I was looking to the people inside the building. I was definitely lost and had a slow leak. Then, I cried "God can you hear me! I am so tired of hurting."So, I decided to leave the abusive marriage that was abusing me emotionally, mentally, verbally, and financially! Enough was enough!

Two weeks after after leaving the toxic relationship, I started to noticing some changes within my body and begin to become nauseous at times while getting headaches frequently. I went to the doctor to find out what was wrong. I found out I was given the best parting gift I could receive. I was almost 4 months pregnant. Okay, now I am in the middle of a broken marriage with 4 kids and living back with my parents. Was this my life? Was I one of those people that would struggle all their life? NO!

A Lady from my church reached out to me asking if I would want to attend her self-love boot camp? I don't have the money, I told her! She then told me that I could be a part of her scholarship program. Every Tuesday, I faithfully called into the classes and with every exercise, I began to smile at myself a little more. I began to love me a little more. I began to love Jesus more! I was falling in love with Jesus again! So I decided that since I had given my heart to a man that broke it multiple times, that I would pick up what remained and give it back to Jesus because He had never broken it but always mended it. The more I worked on the inner me, the happier I became! I then began to look in the mirror, into the eyes of a Queen that was learning how to love herself again. I wanted my outside to reflect the change I felt on the inside. All I needed was some direction. I always had a hard time losing weight so I needed to try something I had never tried before. I signed up with a personal trainer, began to eat right and slowly the weight began to fall off. I was getting my life back and was being the Queen I was always meant to be. After losing over a 150 lbs, I began gaining control of my life and teaching my kids how to overcome. I now had to carry myself as royalty and I was smiling again. The gentleman I divorced is slowly finding a relationship with Christ and is also learning how to love himself. Through all the hurt and pain, Jesus received the glory and I learned as a Queen, not to look back because I was no longer going that way!

Shameka Austin

I plan to make my shift by:

_____

_____

_____

_____

_____

_____

_____

_____

_____

_____

_____

_____

_____

_____

_____

_____

FITNESS
SHIFT PASS
FITNESSSHIFT.COM

"THE ROAD TO HEALTH
AND WELLNESS BEGINS
WITH EDUCATION."

-Shadonne Harris

shadonne@balancedbodymassagegroup.com

12

Miseducation of the Skinny Fat Girl

"Love your body and teach your mind how to respect it"

—SHADONNE HARRIS

As I reflect over my life, looking back over my 3 career changes, the love and support of my spouse of 20 years, two growing children, financial and mental state, and most of all my health and wellness. I asked myself: Are you happy with your life? Would you consider yourself successful..are you thriving spiritually and mentally..and are you healthy? Overwhelmed with mixed emotions…I answered yes with a humble and grateful heart. But what about the rest of your family, sista-friends, and clients that struggle silently and cry in the dark from deteriorating health…I feel burdened to share the message of optimal health because we cannot fulfill our destiny on earth with poor health. So, my heart especially bleeds for my Skinny Fat girls. I was once where you are.

My unhealthy lifestyle began around age 18 when I left Mama Diane's house and decide to eat whatever whenever I wanted!! Breakfast started with croissant, eggs, bacon, or hotcakes, fried apples and could end with Shrimp Scampi from my favorite restaurant—Cheesecake Factory.

I was convinced that I ate healthy because I ate "veggies" or a salad daily. I was misguided into thinking I was healthy because I wore a size "8" which was considered the ideal "sista" weight..cause Lord knows you don't want to be "too small."

As I continued my lifestyle of poor and unbalanced eating and inconsistent exercise, my body begin to breakdown..and breakdown fast! 10 years later I found myself, sporting size 12 clothing, swollen feet, an array of digestive issues along with high cholesterol. When I really think back of that time of my life, my body consistently showed me signs of distress with constant headaches, indigestion, irregular bowel movements just to name a few.

Our bodies always gives us signs. Most times we either choose to ignore them, or not in sync with our bodies, or totally unaware of the warning signs of deteriorating health all together. Healthy living is truly a lifelong journey, beginning with self-awareness and education, mainly won by having a balanced diet and enjoying adequate exercise.

During my pregnancy with the youngest child, the health challenges worsened. We know pregnancy can magnify and bring out any preexisting conditions. On a hot summer in July day, Whitney decided to make her grand entrance into the world a week earlier. I went into the hospital for the one pre-planned C-section to leave with two more surgeries.

The third day after delivering Whitney, I was preparing for discharge. However, I started vomiting uncontrollably shortly after lunch. I was not greatly alarmed, I was thinking it could have been something I ate that did not agree with my stomach and needed to run its course. Well..it was 2 days later and I was still vomiting, and still unable to leave the hospital! The hospital staff performed every test possible but still had no clue. As each day passed, I began to lose confidence and hope in the medical system that I desperately wanted to fix my poor health.

After three days, and plenty of prayers from family and friends..a different doctor came in and said "Have we checked her gall bladder?" She could see my pain and anguish and took it upon herself to wheel me downstairs for a CT scan. A few hours later, the test results were in. They determined my gallbladder had to be removed immediately.

I was both scared and hopeful, wanting to feel better and wanting to return to the comfort of my home. So, the gallbladder surgery was performed that night. As I laid in recovery the next day, I was trying to figure out how long I was in the hospital. It felt like months! In my mind, I was thinking, "I came here to deliver a baby. That's it!"

It seemed as if the delivery room wing was empty and I was the only soul left. I said to the nurse, "Am I the longest person that has stayed here after delivery?" She smiled and said, "Actually no you are not, there was a lady that had a heart attack during delivery and was in the hospital for 30 days." After her response, I began to feel hopeful and grateful about all the chaos that was going on with my health.

The turning point in my life was during the recovery phase in the hospital. A senior doctor was completing his rounds, stopped by to ask how I felt following the surgery. I responded that I felt better but would feel substantially better when you all stopping giving me so many different medications. He gently smiled and responded, "Yes sometimes we make things worse before we make them better."

That statement from the head doctor shook me and I was left with a feeling of hopelessness. For the first time in my life, I realized that my health is solely my responsibility which begins and end with no one else but ME!

Days following the surgery, I had plenty of time to reflect on my health. I pondered on how I made it here and how to make sure I was never in this position again. So, I began to research gallbladder problems. I discovered that some gallbladder problems stem from diets high in fat and cholesterol also while low in fiber. Galatians 6:7 came to my spirit immediately, "Do not be deceived: God is not mocked, for whatever one sows, that will he also reap." I unknowingly sowed years of poor eating choices. Ignorance is never an excuse and healthy living begins with education.

My best friend, Donna gave me the nickname "Skinny Fat Friend" because I was the small frame girlfriend with a pudgy stomach that appeared to look healthy and definitely did not need to "lose" any weight. Instead, I was the miseducated skinny fat girl who felt like I could eat anything I wanted, whenever I wanted without any boundaries. I was truly deceived. There is no such thing!

Well the dilemma or stereotype with us skinny fat women is that we don't have any health issues because we are not visibly overweight. We also struggle in bad relationships with food, lack of exercise, and other health conditions. We just go under the radar and in fact are quite dismissed or ridiculed by friends and family when we embark upon a healthy lifestyle. I often hear, "Girl what do you have to lose?" As a result, we suffer silently as our health declines.

I often times advise my running clients not to get size confused with health. Sadly majority of our health issues are self-inflicted due to our poor eating choices and habits.

During that time of my life, I thought my decline in health was the worst thing that could happen to me. In fact it was these course of events that shifted my destiny and motivated me to help other skinny fat women.

My Success began where my failure ended when I realized I could take back my health. The journey began with education. I researched and applied various holistic approaches until I found a great fit for me.

My first cousins, Lashawn and Dionnah convinced me running would help us lose the fat! So, I starting running in my early 30's, completing 2 marathons and 6 half marathons. Running became my favorite sport. I love that running is a way I can be competitive with myself for my entire life and gain a sense of accomplishment every time I put my shoes on and hit the pavement.

I soon discovered that I needed to include my mind and spirit in order to achieve the ultimate balance of health and wellness. This requires me to always begin and end my day with prayer and meditation. My diet consist of fruit, vegetables, complex carbs, and mostly fish. I feel and look better in my 40's than in my 20's. I am proud to have stayed within 10lbs of my ideal weight for over 14 years (yes my youngest child is now 14 years old). Even with the challenges of having one kidney and no gallbladder I still manage to maintain optimal health.

So, are you the skinny fat girl suffering with deteriorating health? Please don't confuse size with good health! So before the doctor officially diagnose you with high blood pressure, diabetes, heart disease or cancer, I urge you to make a change today. I encourage you to surround yourself with a group of empowering women that will can educate, impart wisdom, and hold you accountable to ensure you reach your fitness goals. The secret to success is to be persistent until you are consistent. You must constantly set new goals.

A wise woman leads change and not allows change to lead her.. otherwise it just may be too late!

I plan to make my shift by:

_____

_____

_____

_____

_____

_____

_____

_____

_____

_____

_____

_____

_____

_____

FITNESS
SHIFT **PASS**
FITNESSSHIFT.COM

"IN ORDER TO BREAK A
BAD HABIT, YOU MUST
WORK TO CREATE A NEW
ONE. YOU ARE THE ONLY
ONE WHO CAN HOLD
YOURSELF ACCOUNTABLE
IN THE END."
-Erin Mercado

purposefilledfitness@gmail.com

13

Take Your Temple Back!

"In order to break a bad habit, you must work to create a new one. You are the only one who can hold yourself accountable in the end."

—ERIN MERCADO

My name is Erin Mercado and this is a short story about my personal journey of overcoming an unhealthy lifestyle and how the Lord gave me the wisdom and determination to reach my fitness goals.

It wasn't until about 2011, weighing about 200 lbs. at 5'6", that I reached a point to where my self-esteem had reached an all-time low and I couldn't bear to look at myself in a photo anymore. I came to the harsh conclusion that deep down I did not love myself and I decided it was finally time to address the issue. I began to ask myself, "What type of body is it that I am really trying to create?" It was then I realized that the body I had did not truly match the "me" on the inside. I knew I would need to make several lifestyle changes in order to see any results. So, I prayed that the Lord would show me what to do and give me the strength to do it.

Like most people, I used food to cope with life; turning towards short-term gratification versus seeking the Lord's help to learn self-control, discipline, as well as learning to love myself the way He does; no strings attached. I had a great relationship with family and friends, but had unintentionally grown distant from the Lord. I was continuously seeking the approval of other people to try and find comfort and confirmation while subconsciously trying to fill the void in my life. I had lost my way and found it easier to receive verbal guidance from trusted loved ones, when what I needed was to find favor through the Lord and work against all of those negative thoughts that had managed to continually find their way back into my life.

The challenge was learning how to look past the weaknesses that once seemed to stand in my way in the past, as they were a constant reminder of my failures. One of my biggest obstacles was the bad habit of eating late at night. During those moments of indulging it always seemed as though I had no will power, and as an outcome, I always woke up with regret the next day. What I had to learn was that while the everyday challenges of life could create roadblocks to making healthy choices, I was not going to let a setback define who I was. I wanted to be healthy and experience life in a more positive way.

I eventually learned self-control and began utilizing resources, such as 'The Daniel Plan', a book written by Rick Warren. These resources, along with guidance from my fiancé, helped me to learn more about myself, the challenges I was facing, and how I could work to form new, healthy habits. It was hard, because the moment I "cheated", I had to overcome the feeling of failure and remind myself that I could still continue on without beating myself up over the bad choice that I had made. I took my first nutrition class at a local community college, to bring me back to the basics and teach me to implement better choices overall. I had to ask myself if the food I was about to eat was going to do anything positive for me. If the answer was no, then I worked hard to avoid it and found healthy alternatives that would help satisfy what my body was craving. It's not about starving yourself or never indulging in a special treat, but it is all about making smarter, healthier choices for yourself. I slowly incorporated moderate exercise, first with the Jazzercise program at a local venue. Over time, I was able to drop over 50 pounds with consistent diet and moderate exercise. After maintaining my ideal weight for a while, I faced a battle, which I had previously overcome, and that was anxiety. My body began to respond to this mental stronghold, consuming my mind with things that would never come to pass. This caused me to not eat properly and I continued to lose weight unintentionally. I realized while the scale measured me at a healthy BMI/weight, I was losing weight in an unhealthy way and knew that I needed to surrender this issue to the Lord, otherwise, I would continue spiraling out of control. This realization motivated me to do more research and learn about how the body operates so that I could make the necessary changes and see how they would affect me personal. Eventually I could incorporate this knowledge in helping others who shared my similar body physique, struggle, and activity level. I made my way back into the gym environment where I started off slow doing basic strength and weight training exercises. If you are just starting and see a "fit" woman in the gym, whose workout seems to be effortless to her, don't become intimidated, as she too had a beginning point and we all have to start somewhere. Never measure yourself up to that of someone else; being "fit" isn't defined by one size or number… it's about being the best YOU can be! The change in my overall mental and emotional state was tremendous.

My husband Alejandro and I have since started a fitness ministry, "Purpose Filled Fitness," where we incorporate calisthenic, cardio, strength, and plyometric conditioning. Our main focus is to reach people in the Southern Maryland area and offer them a place to come and fellowship while encouraging one another to reach their personal fitness goals, and teaching the love of the Lord. I used those principles to prepare for my wedding day in September of 2015, where I achieved my ultimate fitness goals since the beginning of my journey! It was wonderful to experience that sense of excitement in knowing that I accomplished what I set out to do with the help of God's grace, my husband, and hard work and dedication.

I think the most amazing thing God revealed to me during this entire experience, is that I am never going to be perfect, but that I can use my personal struggles to help minister to others and that He might bring someone into our life that might be inspired to find out what God's purpose is for their life as well. With the mercy and strength from the Lord's Word, encouragement of friends and family, and hard work and determination, I was able to successfully make small victories each month; gaining results, progress, self-fulfillment, and knowledge that I could implement into our ministry.

I am still learning that the food I eat, dictates my performance throughout the day; whether at home, work, or at the gym. The more aware we are of the food we eat, the more in tune we become with our bodies, our mental health and our well being. I had to remind myself, "My body is a temple and I should only put good things in it." So yes, living a healthier lifestyle does require being disciplined and living more of a structured lifestyle, but with time, practicing better choices will become a healthy habit and one you can learn to maintain and implement in all walks and stages of your life. I try to remember the strength that Daniel showed, as he persevered in practicing discipline, endurance, devotion, as well as dedication.

If you are struggling with temptation and food addiction, feelings of insecurity or doubt, anxiety/depression, or are curious to see how far you can push yourself to achieve what seems to be the impossible, you should feel empowered in knowing that there are others out there who can relate and that you are not alone. There are so many various contributors to why we use food as a coping mechanism instead of for fuel and they can have a negative impact on us subconsciously. Sometimes, the environments we were raised in, our cultures, and circumstances serve as contributors to our issues. That is why it is important to surround yourself with positive, like-minded people who can support you and encourage you to become the best person that you can be. Having a support group can have such a positive impact on your life and can change your everyday perspective not just about food, but also about yourself as a person. "We are many parts of one body and we all belong to each other" (Romans 12:5). Set the pace for someone else to follow! As I reach a new chapter in my life as a wife and first time mother, I realize now more then ever that I need to embrace my community, as I want to experience a deeper communion and develop a more radical level of friendship with those who genuinely are passionate about loving one another. "We are in this fight together" (Philippians 1:30)!

My best advice is to always put God first because nothing we achieve is by our strength, but by God's grace and purpose. Always work to strive to fulfill a new goal; a healthy lifestyle is never a destination, but a journey! Give your desires to the Lord and ask Him to help direct and guide you to a life that is pleasing to Him. God rewards those who rely on Him! TAKE YOUR TEMPLE BACK!

I plan to make my shift by:

_____

_____

_____

_____

_____

_____

_____

_____

_____

_____

_____

_____

_____

_____

_____

FITNESS
SHIFT PASS
FITNESSSHIFT.COM

"THE DISTANCE BETWEEN
YOUR VISION AND YOUR
MANIFESTATION IS YOUR
ACTION."

-Tiffany Edmonds

tiffanykmusic@aol.com

14

What Are You Weighting For... Just Do It!

"Until your mind shifts, your life won't change"
—Tiffany K Edmonds

Stop! Ask yourself this question: "What am I weighting for?" Think to yourself, "This could be me writing my story." Whatever has stopped you from starting or kept you from finishing, do not allow it. Being an author in this book does not make me any more special than you. The difference is that I decided, one day, to do something different—to change the results I wanted to see in my life.

I'm a wife of 17 years and mom of two, 15 and 12 years old. I am also known as the Happy Chic because I spread happiness everywhere I go. I used to think that was a small thing until I realized that there are so many people who need a breath of fresh happy. So, if I can just say or do something that can redirect their day, It's worth it. Everything I do has a 'happy' seasoning on it. I would, without a doubt, infuse it into every aspect of my life. Music, fashion, and inspiration are some ways I would spread happiness in an effort of bringing joy to those around me.

I am a worship leader, recording artist, and CEO/ Founder of the Studio Me Program. It's a program that jumpstarts the dreams of 6th -12th grade students aspiring to be recording artists. I am also a fashion entrepreneur. When people look good, they feel good. I believe in uplifting and encouraging others in order to give hope in such a hard world. This is just a snippet of who I am.

Before you come to the conclusion that you are unable to shift because you are too busy, read this again. Grab your favorite tea or beverage as I share with you my journey that has the ability to shift you, whether physically, emotionally, mentally, financially, or educationally. What are you weighting for? Let's get it!

The reason I chose "weighting" instead of "waiting" is because we all experience moments in our lives where we become weighted down by life. It could be past hurt, failure, low self-esteem and the list goes on. Sometimes, we don't even know how much weight we are carrying until we lose it. As women, we are nurturers. It is easy to take care of everybody else and disregard our own needs. This keeps us from self care and dealing with own challenges.

I have never had major issues with low self esteem or believing I could do anything, but, I didn't know just how bold and confident I could be until I lost weight. Losing weight created a champion mindset and voice within me that I didn't know existed. As stated before, I have two babies who left me with this thing I call a "pooch pouch". Yes! That thing. You may be high-fiving me right now saying, "I know what you mean, girl." What caused the shift in my mindset? I came to a point where I was tired of it and was ready to see some change.

The interesting part about my story is that I didn't know how much I was challenged until after I lost weight. For years, I ate fried foods, fast foods, and junk foods. I was very consistent in packing on bread, sodas, high carb foods. You could not get me to drink water. Of course in my younger years, it did not seem to affect me or my body. In my mind, I was healthy. After all, I was only a size 10-12, which is considered average, but my doctor prescribed blood pressure medicine for me. She never really emphasized how my eating habits could be a contributing factor to high blood pressure. So, there was no sense of urgency in my mind concerning it. Unhealthy eating was just an everyday occasion for me. This went on for years until I decided I was really ready for change.

Early 2013, I began to inquire about what I could do to get rid of the "pooch pouch" or at least most of it. I thought about a tummy tuck but did not want to go to that extreme. I consulted with an "It Works" distributor and she was honest enough to say, "If you don't change your eating habits, it will defeat the purpose." I also spoke with two fitness trainers that said the same thing basically. "If you don't eat healthy, working out won't work." "Belly fat is mostly what you eat. You have to change your eating habits." I needed to make a conscious decision to change. Until you get intentional, nothing will happen on purpose.

On April 2013, I started the Body by Tosha detox plan weighing in at 161 lbs. I looked over the plan and modified it to a doable goal for me. I wanted it to be a lifestyle change and not just a 30-day diet. I am a huge breakfast eater, so giving up biscuits, pancakes, pork sausage and pork bacon was challenging. I cannot even express the love I had for those things. LOL! I did that consistently for years and remained the same weight. That means, what you do consistently will work, good or bad. I didn't think I could live without my big breakfast. I had to change the way I thought about food in order to change my eating habits. It was not as hard as I thought it would be. I shifted from dumb eating to smart eating.

BBT offered a great support system where accountability partners shared various meal ideas. As I continued the plan, it became a habit. I saw a difference literally in 3 days just by eating smarter. At the end of the 30 days, I lost 17 lbs and much belly fat. Praise Jesus! Lol! My goal was to lose belly fat by eating better, but my results far exceeded my reason. Results are at the end of your follow through. It's been three years now and I am still within my weight window.

Yes, get you a weight window. I don't like saying my goal is 140lbs and that's it. If I don't reach 140lbs, then I'm not happy? No, I gave myself a weight window of 136 to 145 lbs. 136lbs was my high school weight and 145 lbs was my weight before pregnancy. I'm still in awe that I changed my life and have remained consistent on this journey.

If you keep waiting to start, you will never start. Those who wait are those who weight. What are you weighting for…Just do it! Get off the weight roller coaster and make a change for life. Your body has had enough already. The sooner you start, the sooner you will be a healthier you. Weight loss is just as mental as it is physical. Until your mind shifts, your life won't change. IF I DID IT, YOU CAN DO IT. I want to push you to get on the road to fitness, health, and wellness. It's time to go to another level of thinking, being, and doing.

Unfortunately, you will never know that it works for you until you do it. If you THINK you can't live without your bread, sodas, chips, etc., then you won't. Stop wishing and hoping and just do the dawgone thang. Can I say "dawgone"? Seriously, it's your life and you have to take control of it. Ain't nobody got time for fat, unhealthy eating, and body abusing. Get your life! And watch the weight fall off. As soon as you change the way you eat and what you eat, the weight will change. What are you weighting for? Start somewhere. Take a walk, play a sport with your kids, park farther away from the store, take the stairs, dance, etc. Don't allow your circumstances to create excuses for you. You may not be able to do what others do, but you have to find out what works for you. "I don't have time to exercise" is really not an excuse, it's an option you choose. I made the mistake of watching others do what they do: gym everyday, run 100 miles everyday, juice everyday, 1 million squats everyday, 50 buckets of water of everyday, etc. you get it!!! And so I counted myself out of the "team healthy" game before I even started. I thought I would or could never be that extreme, but I had to start where I was. I had to stop comparing myself and stop canceling myself out. You can't compare your beginning to someone's ending. I learned how to use their journeys as inspiration to actually begin my own. I had to start and it is really that simple. Mind over matter.

The next time you go to the store or mall, park as far away as you can and walk. Make small changes that will produce big results. Effort leaves a trail of evidence. Let those calories add up, the movement will add up. Let's add movement and subtract the weight.

The greatest part of my journey was gaining an new awareness of who I was. I had no idea that it would open me up to such wellness and spiritual being. I was never really an emotional person and definitely not a crier. But now, I am more connected to not just my emotions but what others feel. It also increased my faith, spiritual awareness, and built strength in me like never before.

In April 2016, our house caught on fire and we lost just about everything. You could not have told me that this would be a part of my story. I stood in the aftermath and declared that I would not faint or lose my faith. I know without a doubt that my weight loss journey was key to my stand. The fire presented itself as a "weight" for me. I had to decide like I did in April 2013 that I was not going to carry that weight. I had to be intentional about my freedom and declare a best come back ever. Every area in our lives connects to another. When you lose weight, it releases you in so many other areas of your life. Once the body, soul, and mind align, you will be unstoppable. What are you weighting for....just do it!

I plan to make my shift by:

_____

_____

_____

_____

_____

_____

_____

_____

_____

_____

_____

_____

If you would like to bring the Fitness Shift movement
to your city, please contact us at:
www.FitnessSHIFT.com

Made in the USA
Charleston, SC
17 October 2016